Dee Caldwell's
book of
freestyle boardsailing

Dee Caldwell's book of freestyle boardsailing

photographs by Tim Hore

with a chapter by Alex Schatunowski

Fernhurst Books

First published 1983 by
Fernhurst Books, 13 Fernhurst Road,
London SW6 7JN

ISBN 0 906754 07 0

Acknowledgements

The publishers gratefully acknowledge the help
of Ten Cate (England) Ltd and the Windsurfer
Class Association GB in the preparation of
this book. Thanks are also due to Alex
Schatunowski for his advice on the manuscript.

The photographs were taken by Tim Hore
at the Grafham Water Residential Centre,
West Perry, Huntingdon, Cambs. and at
Princes Waterski Club, Ashford, Middlesex,
and thanks are due to both centres for their
hospitality.

The cover photograph is by David Edmund-
Jones and the cover design is by Behram
Kapadia.

Composition by Allset, London
Printed by Butler & Tanner Ltd, Frome

Contents

The right equipment

It is perfectly possible to do freestyle on any board, but it is much easier if you have the right equipment.

The board. The ideal board for freestyle has rounded rails, to give a good grip when rail-riding. Choose one with a flat bottom (for stability) and the right volume for your weight — excessive volume hinders manoeuvrability as does a long waterline length. The deck should be non-slip over most of its surface with no ridges — there are plenty of ways of falling off without tripping over a bump in the skin.

The skeg. Cut off part of the skeg to help the board turn.

Freestyle skeg (left); normal skeg (right).

The daggerboard. The most important thing about the daggerboard is that it should stay in position. For example, for some tricks it's helpful to raise the daggerboard so that part of it sticks up from the deck, giving you something to grip with your foot.

In strong winds raise the daggerboard or use a smaller one.

The mast. Use a fibreglass mast — this material is lighter than alloy and easier to pull out of the water.

The sail. Choose the correct sail size for the conditions — in most winds 5.7 m² is fine but I change down to a 4.2 m² in strong winds. Your freestyle sail should have a high clew (to prevent it dragging in the water) and be short at the bottom of the mast. Sails like this are easier to duck underneath and don't sweep your feet off the board as the boom swings across.

Tying the inhaul. I like to wind the inhaul around the mast several times in case the knot slips. Then lay the boom along the mast and pull the inhaul tight. When the boom is swung back to its proper position the inhaul should be as tight as possible without damaging the mast. Test this by lifting up the mast — the inhaul should support the boom horizontally.

The universal joint. Check that the joint is pivoting freely; usually you will need to clean sand out of it. The universal joint must not come out of the board. If the fit is poor, wrap tape around the flange and hammer it home, being careful not to split the board.

Tying the outhaul. Outhaul cleats halfway down the boom are a menace in freestyle so move them to the back. Pull the outhaul tight to get rid of most of the curve in the sail, cleat the rope and tidy the ends around the boom.

The outhaul.

1

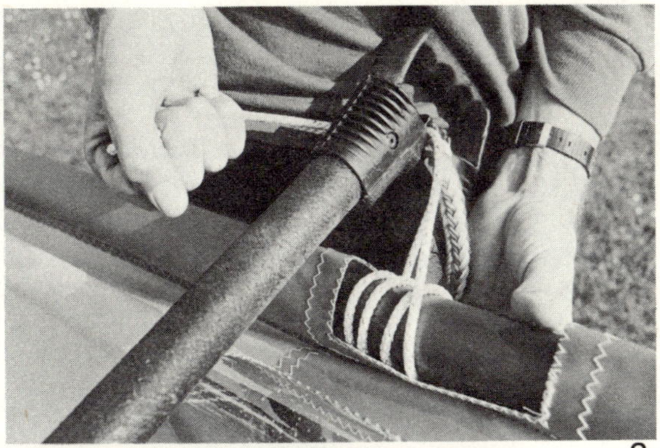

2

3

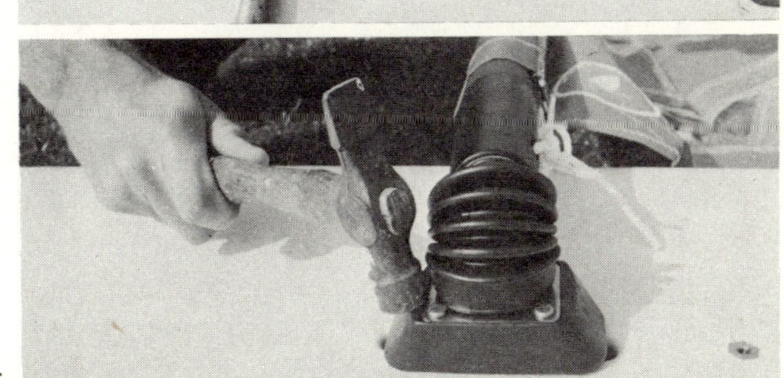

4

5

Tying the inhaul. (1) The inhaul should support the
boom horizontally. (2) Wind the inhaul around the
mast several times; it should be as tight as possible
without damaging the mast (3).
Improve the fit of the universal joint by wrapping the
flange with tape (4) and hammering it home (5).

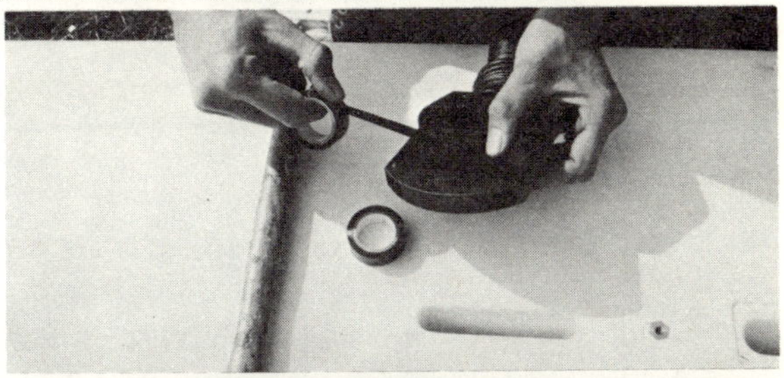

Wax. Use soft surf wax to give a grip on the rails, the glossy parts of the deck (such as transfers) and the daggerboard.

Clothing. You must be able to move freely so make sure the arms of your jacket are loose-fitting. Choose shoes that grip and wear shin pads for railriding practice. If you wear spectacles, tie them on firmly with neoprene strips — they will then float if disaster strikes!

Terms used in this book. The photograph shows the terms used for the various parts of the board and rig. The terms 'mast hand' and 'sail hand' are also used except where it is too confusing: then 'right hand' and 'left hand' are used to correspond with the photo sequence demonstrating a particular trick. To perform the trick on the opposite tack, read 'left' for 'right' and vice versa.

Parts of the board.

Practising ashore

Most of the tricks in this book can be practised ashore. A beginner to freestyle should probably spend half his or her time practising on the beach and half on the water. Even an expert will profit from a ten-minute workout on land before going afloat. It is far easier to pro-gramme yourself to do a trick properly if a mistake only means stepping onto the sand rather than a ducking. And one thing is certain — if you can't do a trick on land you certainly will not be able to do it on the water.

Practising with the board flat. Rig the board in the usual way but without the daggerboard or skeg. If possible, practise in a gentle breeze: a steady force 2 is ideal.

Before you align your board relative to the wind, decide which is the key part of the trick you are going to practise. In a duck tack, for example, the essence of the trick is ducking under the sail as the board turns through the wind — so position your board nose to wind. For tricks such as back to sail, point the board across the wind (on a reach).

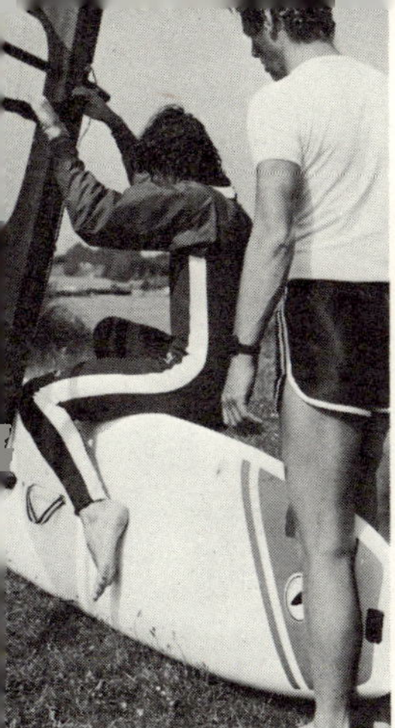

Practising railriding on dry land: with the board held firmly, raise yourself into position.

When you are steady, your helper can relax his grip. All the while balance by sheeting out and pressing on the daggerboard, or by sheeting in.

Practising tricks on the rail. Insert the daggerboard and align the board across the wind. Set it on the rail and ask a friend to support it between his knees. If you don't have a helper handy, a set of posts will do.

You can't simulate flipping the board on edge, but you can practise the position you are aiming for just after the flip. Sit on the board with one thigh on the rail and the other foot on the daggerboard. If the board tips towards you, pull in with your sail hand. If the board tips away from you, spill wind with your sail hand and kick down on the daggerboard. When you are confident, raise yourself to the railride position by stepping up on your front foot and pulling down on the boom. Your back foot goes on the rail — when you are railriding on the water you use this foot to keep the board going straight. Balance as before; you will find it easier to begin with if the board is touching the mast but as you improve a gap will open up. Now you are ready for your helper to relax his grip on the board and finally to let you ride the rail alone.

Practice sessions afloat. During your practice sessions you should always run through your whole repertoire. Then concentrate on one trick; when you get fed up or tired, stop — or go back and practise on land. Keep in mind the key feature of each trick; once you have mastered this, everything else will follow.

Practising a duck tack.

Practising back to sail.

1   Sailing inside boom

This trick became very popular in the Wind-surfer class before harness lines were allowed as it enabled you to rest your arms in a strong wind, while still sailing. You stand inside the boom with your back leaning against it and arms resting on it. There's no need to practise this on dry land. Go out in a very light wind and try it: it won't be long before you have graduated to medium winds.

1   Sailing across the wind, pass your sail hand underneath the boom and grasp it in the same place but from the other side with your wrist twisted. Grab the mast with your mast hand.

2   Lean forward and lower your head underneath the boom until the boom is lying on the nape of your neck. Practise getting in and out of this position a few times before moving on.

3   Now stand up between the boom and the sail with the boom against the top of your back. Let your back take the pressure of the rig and lean farther back the stronger the wind. Steer by raking the mast in the usual way.

4   When confident, bring the mast hand underneath the boom, also holding it from the wrong side. If the wind is strong you can hold the mast just under the boom. You can lift your elbows and drop them over the boom, as shown here, but don't do this when conditions are gusty — you may want to get out of the position quickly. To abort just lean forward, drop your head and bend your knees, letting the boom pass overhead — and remembering to catch it!

Remember . . .
. . . when inside the boom just duck your head and stick your bottom out to get out of trouble.
. . . try to get the boom as far down your back as possible to avoid getting tired.

Change grip with your sail hand (step 1).

Mistake: be positive — the whole body should be
inside the boom, not just the neck!

An embellishment to this trick is to stand with both feet behind the mast.

This comparatively easy trick looks great when done in strong winds. With enough practice you can lean right back into the sail and balance the rig against your back without using your hands. Back to sail is important because it is used in many of the more difficult tricks. Begin in a steady force 2 — in lighter winds you will have problems balancing with nothing to lean back against.

1   Sailing on a reach, sheet out and when ready pass your sail hand round to the other side of the boom.

2   Hold the rig in this position with the mast hand by your side until confident. Your front foot should be 15 cm in front of the mast, your back foot 15 cm behind.

3   Now pull the rig to windward at the same time moving your back foot round in front of the mast and onto the daggerboard case, catching the mast behind your back with your mast hand.

4 Lean back into the sail and shift your sail hand farther along the boom away from the mast. The pressure should be mainly on your mast hand, not your back. When confident, bring the front foot behind the mast as well.

5 Once under way the position is easier to hold but remember when the wind gusts to twist your body around towards the nose of the board which will allow you to sheet out but stay back to sail.

6 To recover, just pivot around on the front foot and grab the other boom.

Remember . . .

. the stronger the wind the more you must lean back into the sail, so that it leans well over to windward.

. . . to step round the mast and lean back into the sail in one movement.

. . . practice on dry land will teach you to handle the gusts, and give you the feeling of leaning to windward.

To recover, step back round the mast like this.

This trick will really confuse the fans on the beach as it looks as though you are sailing backwards. It is not a very efficient form of sailing but it's interesting and a real challenge in strong winds. The objective is to reverse the roles of the mast and the leech of the sail. Getting into a clew-first position in strong winds is difficult but once that is mastered the rest of the trick is easy.

1 Begin by sailing across the wind. When you're ready, let go with your mast hand (right hand in the photo sequence) and shift it well back along the boom, simultaneously letting go with your left hand. The mast will begin to fall towards the water.

2 Now pull the rig to windward and towards the nose of the board with your right hand.

3 Let go with your right hand and grab the other side of the boom with both hands. Your right hand is now nearest the clew of the sail.

4 If you pull in with your left hand the sail will fill. Try to think of the leech as the mast and hold it steady. When the wind gusts let the mast turn to leeward, spilling wind.

5 To return to normal sailing let the boom swing round to leeward, pulling the mast to windward to keep the clew out of the water.

Remember . . .
. . . that because the curve in the sail is back to front it is harder than usual to spill wind so keep a tight grip with your right hand.
. . . to hold the boom with your hands wider apart than usual which will help you control the rig.
. . . if the boom is pulled out of your right hand pull the mast up as the sail flicks round in order to keep the clew out of the water.

Although this is not a difficult trick to learn, once it can be performed well in strong winds it will be a crucial part of the more complicated tricks and will also improve your overall boardsailing ability. When you are racing, for example, it is very useful to be able to sail backwards competently on the start line.

Unfortunately you can't really practise this trick on dry land, so it is best to start off in a gentle force 1 or 2 and then build up to stronger winds.

There are two ways of doing this trick. The first is to sheet out when sailing across the wind and wait for the board to stop; then simply treat the stern of the board as the front and sail off backwards, looking the way you're going. The second way, shown in the photo sequence, is to brake and reverse when you're going full tilt, which is naturally more spectacular.

1   Sail across the wind with the stern of the board pointing the way you will want to go.

2   Transfer your mast hand (left hand in the photo sequence) to the mast and let the sail swing to leeward. Then place your new front foot in front of the mast, put most of your weight on it and sheet in with both hands.

3   The board will become very twitchy, more so as you pick up speed because the skeg is now acting as a 'front rudder'. Steer by pushing with your front foot to turn away from the wind; rake the mast back (and pull the boom in) to turn towards the wind.

4   When you can manage to sail backwards in a strong wind, try spinning the board 180° and sailing off bow-first again. While sailing backwards the stern is constantly trying to turn into the wind; simply allow it to do so and encourage it to swivel further by some nifty footwork.

Remember . . .

. . . to use your feet as well as the rig to steer.

5 Flare gybe

This trick is useful when racing as it allows you to approach the gybe mark at speed and then slow the board right down by jumping back, gybing at the same time. Control on the run is one of the main problems in board-sailing, and this trick helps you to stay on the board by showing you how to steer by tilting the board rather than by shifting the rig around.

The objective is to gybe by jumping to the back of the board, depressing the stern into the water and letting the nose come out. You can then turn the board and sail around at the same time.

1 Set off on a broad reach in a medium wind with the daggerboard down as far as possible without the board railing.

2 Now jump or step very quickly to within half a metre of the back of the board. Keep holding the rig firmly and the nose will tilt out as you pull on the rig.

3 Keep your weight evenly on both feet to start with. When ready to turn depress the windward rail more than the leeward rail and the board will swivel round. The speed of this depends on how hard you depress the rail.

4 As you turn the board with your feet lean forward and the board will flatten out slightly. This helps the board turn. Once the board position is where you want it step quickly up the board with your outside foot,

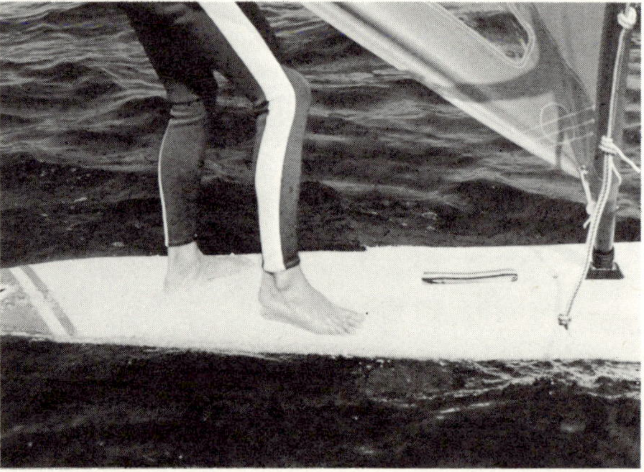

Mistake: my weight should be further back, and the right foot should be back and pressing down.

releasing the boom with the sail hand. The sail will then flick round pivoting on the mast hand.

5   Once the sail is directly downwind shift the old sail hand onto the mast just below the boom and rake the mast forwards (to stop the board turning further) and to windward (to keep the clew out of the water). At the same time let go with the old mast hand and shift it to the other side of the boom. Pull in and sail off.

Remember . . .

. . . when you complete the gybe, lean back as the board accelerates.

. . . division II round boards have more volume especially at the back and really need sinking. Keep your feet wrapped round both rails for more control.

. . . to have the daggerboard down as far as you can get away with.

. . . that depressing one rail more than the other makes the board turn away from the side that is depressed.

Step back and push right; then use your feet to control the board as it turns. Finally move forwards to kill the turn.

6 Nose sink

You must be able to sail downwind competently and to sail backwards in order to stand a chance of completing this trick. The **flare gybe** steering technique can also be used once the nose has sunk beneath the water.
It is difficult to practise this trick on land but you can get the feel of stepping back to the nose of the board and sheeting in at the same time. To do this place the board nose to wind on the sand in a medium wind. Then try to sheet in and step to the nose of the board. Lean back hard to take the pressure of the wind in the rig. You may find you need some wax on the nose transfer especially when this gets wet.

The objective is to sail downwind standing on the nose of the board pressing it into the water so that the skeg and most of the daggerboard come out of the water—and then recover!

1 You can either start at rest or turn into the wind as if to tack (as in the photo sequence). As the board comes head to wind with the sail flapping, step around the mast and use your feet to get the board pointing on a 'backwards' broad reach.

2 Sheet in and at the same time step quickly onto the nose of the board so that the stern lifts out. To begin with step back just enough to bring the skeg out as this will allow you to steer and control the board.

3 As the stern of the board comes up depress the windward rail and the board will swivel round. Stop depressing once the board is straight downwind and bring the rig across the board as if you were on a run.

4 To steer, combine tilting the board with your feet and leaning the rig from side to side.

5   Keep your arms bent, leaning the rig back towards you. If you feel you're sinking too much or the wind drops, simply straighten your arms and the rig will become more powerful, pulling you forwards. Take this opportunity to step nearer the mast.

Remember . . .
. . . to bring the rig towards you when stepping back in case the wind gusts.
. . . always keep the skeg out of the water as it increases manoeuvrability.
. . . it is possible to do this trick in strong winds as most of the power can be taken out of the rig by leaning it well to windward.
. . . you can also get into the nose sink by pointing the stern downwind, sheeting in and jumping back at the same time, although this requires a lot of confidence.

7 Sailing leeward side of sail

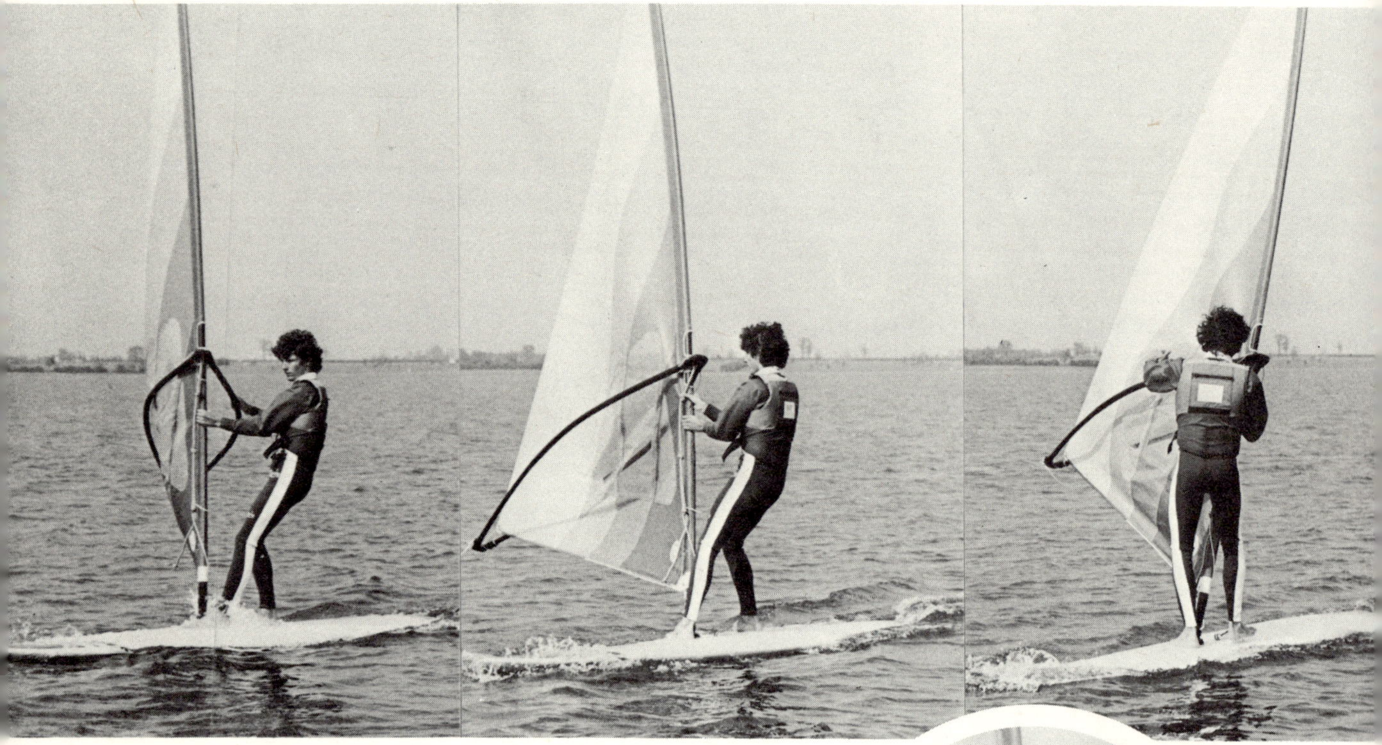

This is the first trick I ever learned and I still practise it, especially in strong winds when it is less tiring than sailing in the normal position. Try this trick in a force 2 to start with; you can practise it on dry land by placing the board across the wind and following the instructions below.

The objective of the trick is to step round the mast while under way and sail on, facing the wind and pushing the boom away from you.

1 Sailing on a beam reach, transfer your mast hand (left hand in this photo sequence) to the mast. When you're ready, take your right hand to the mast too.

2 Take small steps round the mast, facing it and leaning it to windward.

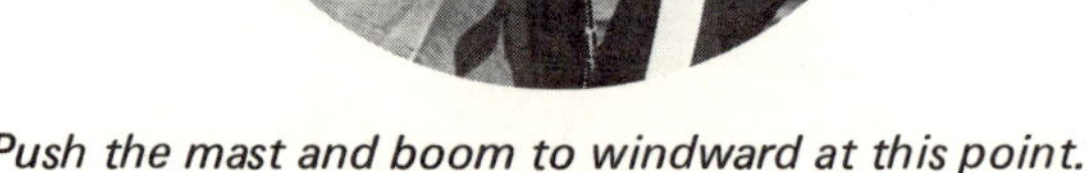

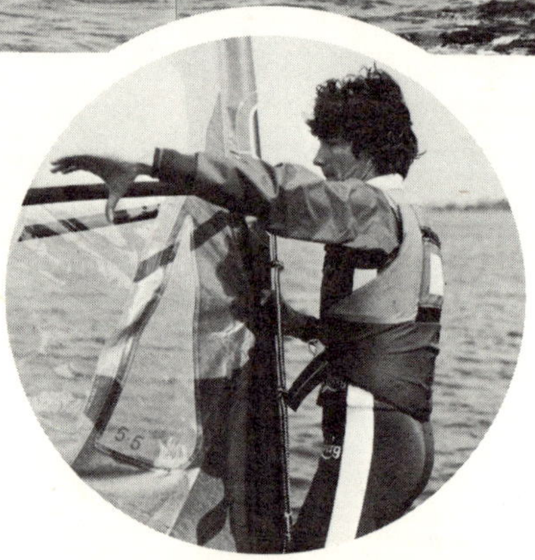

Push the mast and boom to windward at this point.

3 Grab the boom with your left hand and push it to windward. At this point you should bring your body fully to the leeward side of the sail and have one foot in front of the mast and the other behind it.

4   Keep your right hand straight initially as you will find the rig hard to hold down. It is here that you must learn to pull your left hand towards you when you want to sheet out (to release pressure on the rig) and away from you to sheet in.

5   Lean your body and the rig to windward to help hold it down and make it more manageable.

6   To return to normal sailing pull in with your left hand, then grab the mast with both hands and step back to the windward side of the rig.

Remember . . .

. . . to move quickly and smoothly so the board remains under way while you complete the manoeuvre.

. . . don't overshoot when on the leeward side of the sail otherwise you will stall the sail.

. . . to lean the mast to the front of the board to prevent it turning into the wind.

In strong winds lock your right arm solid to help hold down the rig.

21

This is perhaps the best known and oldest trick in boardsailing. A great trick to learn in the early stages of freestyle as it takes a bit of courage to force yourself to lean out to windward and dip your head into cold water. Unfortunately, you can't practise this on land.

1   A steady medium-to-strong wind helps when learning as you can lean further out and over the water. Start sailing across the wind and keep your hands fairly wide apart on the boom.

2   Extend your arms to keep the rig as upright as possible.

3   Now ease out your sail hand slightly and lean your head back until it is touching the water — only hold the position for a split second to start with. Pull in with your sail hand and the extra power in the rig will lift you up again.

4   You can head dip in lighter wind by bending your knees and getting your weight further over the board as there is then less weight for the rig to hold up. Holding the mast below the boom also helps and you can even head dip sitting on the board holding the mast and the bottom of the sail.

5   When holding the head dip for a while beware of the board luffing up into the wind otherwise you will fall into the water.

Remember . . .
. . . if in trouble, bend your knees to get your weight off the rig and back onto the board.
. . . to learn in a strong wind to start with.

This trick starts off just like an ordinary **back to sail**; you then duck inside the boom and lean back against the leeward side of the sail. To finish this trick off neatly duck out again, then move your body round the mast ready for the next trick.

Practise this trick on dry land in a light wind until you understand the movements. Place the board across the wind and have the inhaul a little slacker than normal to allow you to twist the boom.

1 Start by getting into a back to sail position (page 12).

2 When confident, tilt the boom up with your sail hand, bend your legs, let the boom swing downwind slightly and duck under it.

3 Now press your body against the sail. The resulting distortion makes the sail easier to hold up in a heavy wind. Keep steering by leaning the rig to and fro with your body.

4 Now move your front foot back behind the mast, and your mast hand inside the boom.

5 To recover, reverse the steps above.

Remember . . .

. . . to push the mast forward and to windward when getting under way.

. . . to raise the boom with your sail hand when ducking underneath.

. . . don't put both arms inside the boom until you're fully confident because it's tricky to recover from this position.

10 Sail 360

This trick really shows what the universal joint is all about as the mast moves all over the place. Having the right freestyle gear makes life easier and the trick is simplified by using a lightweight mast.

The object is to spin the sail through 360° while on the move. A useful tip — try it while reaching and surfing down a wave as the sail is then easier to flick round. As the board travels down the wave the pressure is taken out of the sail and so some of the work is done for you.

1 Begin by sailing across the wind. Let go of the boom with your mast hand (right hand in this photo sequence), cross it over the left hand and grab the boom again near the clew of the sail.

2 As the mast falls towards the water let go with your left hand and drop it to your side for a second.

3 Just before the mast touches the water pull the rig clew-first upwards and forwards and let go with your right hand.

4 Grab the mast with your left hand halfway between the boom fixing and universal joint and pull it towards you, at the same time using your right hand to push the sail window away from you and towards the front of the board. The wind will now catch the sail and flick it round. Let the mast swivel in your left hand and bring it upright which will stop the clew hitting the water. Finally sheet in and continue sailing.

Remember . . .
. . . to grab the boom as far up towards the clew of the sail as possible.
. . . to tug the rig to windward as far as possible.
. . . stop the clew from hitting the water by pulling the mast to an upright position.

Mistake: pull the boom up at this point or the sail will hit the water as it spins round.

This trick looks great when done successfully in a strong wind, especially if you can then turn it into a 720.

The object here is to do a **sail 360** but follow the rig round with your body. A different procedure is needed from that used for an ordinary sail 360. Try it either on the beach or in very light winds until your hands and feet are positioned correctly and then it should be relatively easy.

1 Sail on a reach with your hands fairly wide apart.

2 Now bring the mast well to windward and push the boom round so the clew is nearest the front of the board.

3 Place your back foot (left foot in this photo sequence) in front of the mast and continue pushing the boom into the wind.

4 As the clew goes through the eye of the wind bring your body round the front of the board.

5 The wind will now catch the sail and swing it round over the back of the board to its original position. Hold on tightly with your right hand and pull the mast to windward slightly to stop the clew hitting the water.

6 In a strong wind it is advisable to let go of the boom with your left hand as it passes over the stern of the board otherwise you run the risk of being pulled forward into the water.

Remember . . .

. . . to lean the mast well to windward before you start pushing the boom round through the eye of the wind.

. . . if you do let go of the boom keep your hand close to it so you can sheet in quickly and get going again (and with luck the judges will never know you let go).

A different viewpoint shows how far you must push the mast to windward in step 2.

12 Spin tack

I personally found that I could never be fully confident with this trick until at last I put the board head to wind on the beach and went very slowly through the manoeuvre using the same steps again and again, then speeding up until it became automatic.

A useful hint is to have the uphaul line held close to the mast with a piece of elastic cord to prevent you getting tangled up in the line.

The object is to tack the board and go round the front of the board doing a 360° turn at the same time. A light breeze and a good grip will make it easier.

1 Tilt the mast back as if to tack but place your mast hand (left hand in this photo sequence) on the mast just below the boom and keep your right hand on the boom until you start to spin.

2 Keep both feet behind the mast until the board comes almost head to wind. Then, releasing your right hand, start to spin round on your left foot, spinning in the direction of the stern of the board first.

3 Place your right foot in front of the mast and release the mast with your left hand. Grab it with your right hand as you continue spinning.

4 Now spin on your right foot and grasp the boom with your left hand. Transfer your right hand to the boom when ready.

Remember . . .
. . . when releasing the mast with your left hand, give it a sharp tug to windward to stop it hitting the water while you spin.
. . . to lean the mast well forward to bear away.

The ideal position halfway through the spin.

Mistake: if you keep both feet behind the mast the rig will force you off the board.

You have to practise getting into position for a nose dip in a light wind but it can only be completed in a medium to strong wind. It is best described as a reverse **head dip**.

You must be able to sail on the windward side of the sail with your back to the boom. Keep trying this in stronger and stronger winds until completely confident. It is difficult to practise on dry land so just start off in a gentle wind.

1 Point the board across the wind with the sail just flapping. Grasp the boom close to the mast with your sail hand and turn your body to face into the wind.

2 Hold this position until you are reasonably confident. Then bring the mast very slightly to windward and reach behind you with your former mast hand and grasp the boom.

3 Now sheet in slightly and extend the new mast hand fully, leaning your body into the wind.

4   Once you are under way the board will tend to luff up unless you lean the mast to the front of the board. Be ready to bring the mast back once you are heading across the wind.

5   To sheet in and out, roll your body. In other words, if you want to sheet out twist to face the stern of the board, and to sheet in turn to face the front.

6   To dip your nose into the water you have to sheet out slightly, bend your knees and bend your head into the water. As your nose hits the water sheet in so that you are pulled back up.

7   If the wind is not strong enough, either place your mast hand on the mast below the boom or bend down on one knee.

Remember . . .
. . . in gusty winds you must sheet out by twisting your body.
. . . don't try to hold the nose dip for long, as the board tends to luff up while you are not looking.
. . . once up, sheet out to stop yourself falling in backwards.

The sequence below shows what happens if you pull the boom across to windward rather than bending your knees.

14 Pirouette

The pirouette is one of the three basic tricks in freestyle; the other two are the **railride** and **sail 360**. It is from these three that most other tricks are devised — variations on a theme.

The pirouette involves spinning the body 360° while still sailing and is a great trick to learn on dry land — I used to practise pirouetting indoors while snow fell outside. Practise with just the board to start with, then try with the rig. When you feel you have the hang of it move onto the water.

1   Start sailing on a beam reach in a light wind. Place your front foot in the middle of the board near the daggerboard case and start to twist your body in a clockwise direction.

2   Push off with the back foot and swivel on the ball of the front foot.

3   Just before you let the boom go sheet out a little and pull the rig to windward so that when you have completed the turn the rig has blown back to the original position.

4   Stop the spin by planting your back foot firmly in its original position and at the same time grabbing the boom with both hands.

5   Once you can do this trick easily in all weather conditions try doing a 720° turn before grabbing the boom.

Remember . . .

. . . it is very important to pull the mast to windward just before going into the pirouette.

. . . to pirouette slowly until you have the hang of it.

. . . almost slap your back foot down when stopping the spin.

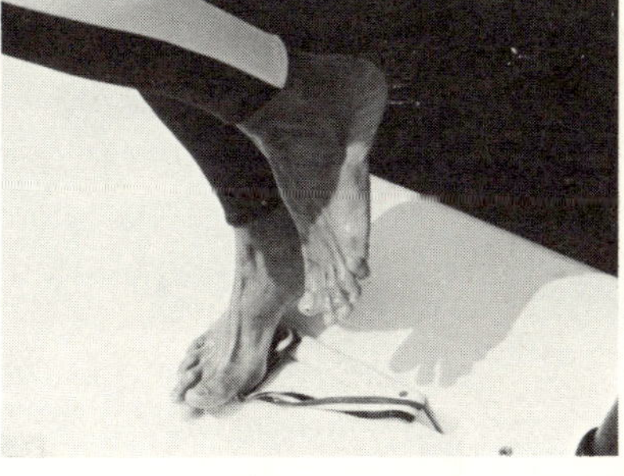

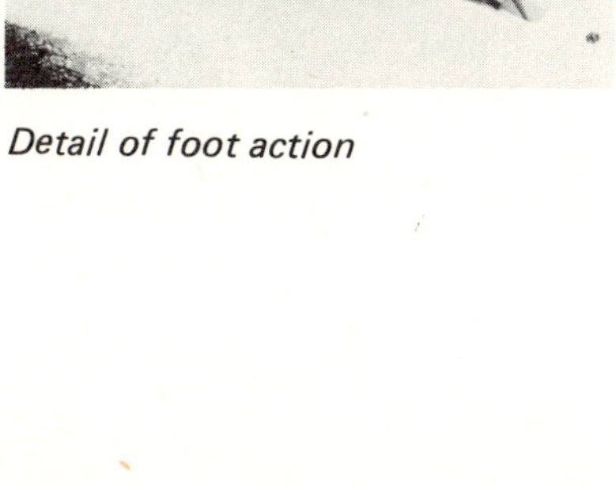

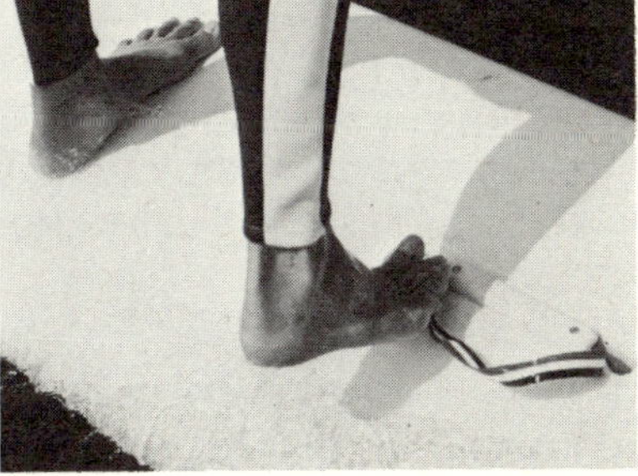

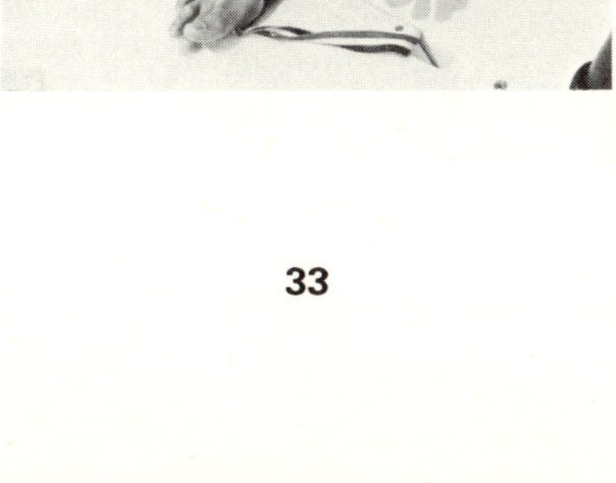

Detail of foot action

15 Water start

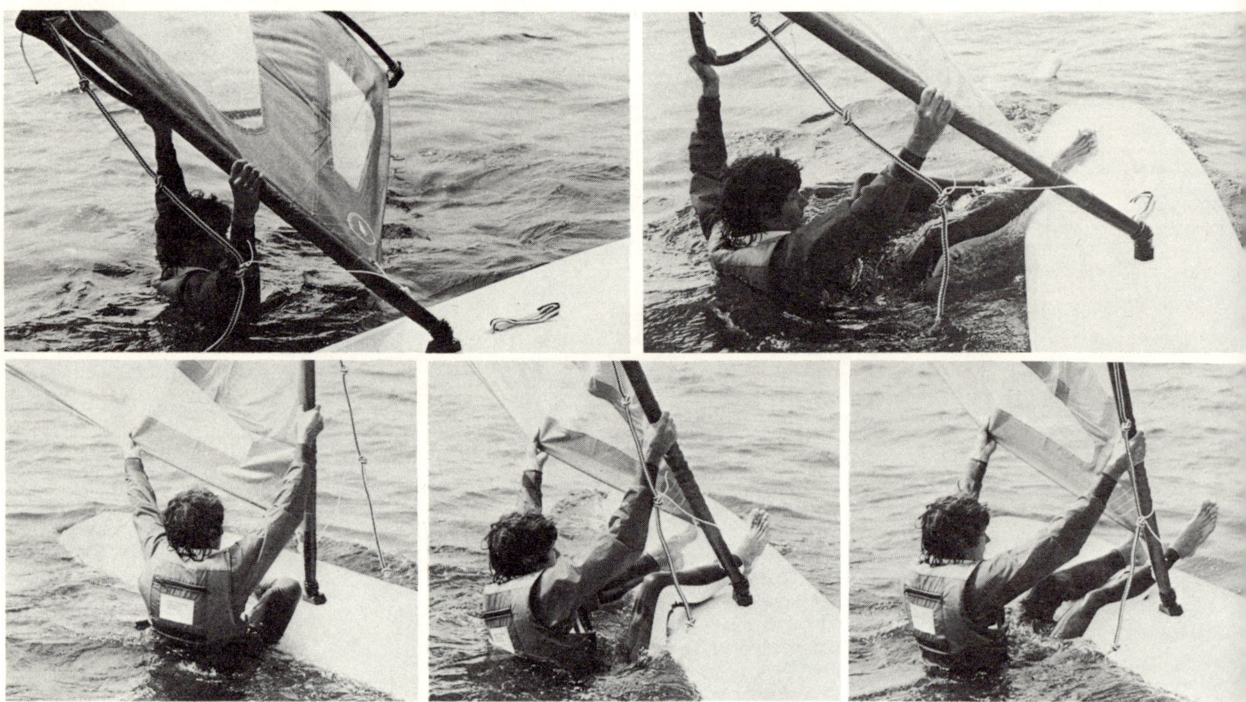

The water start is one of the most useful tricks to learn if you are a high-wind sailor or small-board jumper as it is often easier to water start in a high wind than to try to pull up the rig, especially on a short board.

For serious racing the water start is a must as often you either have your feet knocked off the board or you hit a dead patch in the wind, both of which leave you in the water to windward of the board with the boom in your hands or the sail fully immersed.

When you start to learn this trick it is important to have the right conditions — a force 4 wind and a shallow bottom so you can stand. As you become more confident move to deeper water.

1 Kneel down in the water and hold the tip of the mast so that the board is blown to leeward. Then hand over hand push the mast into the air and let the rig catch the wind. As it moves out of the water grab the boom.

2 Just hold the rig in this position. The stronger the wind the more you pull the rig down towards you. In lighter wind straighten your arms. It's very important to grasp the idea that the more vertical the rig, the more power it has to lift you out of the water. Practise this until you feel you have complete control of the rig.

3 Now place both feet on the side of the board and push it around until it is side-on to the wind by bending and straightening your legs and raking the mast fore and aft. The leg-work will help you control the rig, as the further your body weight is from the board the easier it is to hold the rig down.

4 Bend your knees slowly and straighten your arms. The rig will move towards an upright position and pluck you from the water. As you are pulled up onto the board, sheet out to avoid being carried straight over.

5 To try a water start without having the rig fully immersed, sail on a beam reach then sheet out and lower your body into the water at the same time. Keep your feet on the side of the board and practise controlling the rig while in the water; then water start out.

Remember . . .

. . . the less wind there is the more you have to straighten your arms. If this is still not enough to push the rig up grasp the mast below the boom with your mast hand and place your calves on the board. In very light

In the sequence above I am trying the most difficult water start — in a very light wind. Holding the boom in both hands gives insufficient power so I try holding the mast and boom which also fails. By transferring my sail hand to the foot of the sail and sliding my legs right across the board I'm able to get the rig vertical. As the rig falls to leeward I pull on it and scramble onto the board. Note the leg-and-sail work in the middle of the sequence to turn the board across the wind.

winds try one hand on the mast and the other on the foot of the sail. This gets the rig vertical for maximum power.

. . . to steer your board by pushing the rig towards the front of the board and away from you to make the nose bear away or pulling it towards you to turn the nose into the wind.

. . . wearing a buoyancy harness makes it less tiring to lift the rig up.

On these two pages I show you how to tail sink as well as catapult. It is important that you can sail downwind competently in a strong wind as this makes it easier to catapult the board.

The only part of this trick that can be practised on dry land is to learn the feel of getting under way when going downwind. To do this place the board stern to wind in the sand and practise sheeting in and stepping back at the same time.

For some reason the tail sink is harder than a **nose sink**, perhaps because the skeg and daggerboard rake backwards and are further in the water. If you have only learned a few tricks the catapult tail sink is a good one to end your routine.

1   Bear off onto a run with (ideally) a steady force 3 or 4 on your back. Rake the rig right back if the wind is stronger than this.

2   Now take two quick steps to the back of the board. Try not to press down too much on either rail or the board will turn violently (in the opposite direction to the rail that has been depressed). Steer by **gently** pressing on the appropriate rail.

3   Keep sliding your feet further down the board if you feel that the wind is strong enough to let you stay on. The objective is to slow the board right down.

4   Keep your arms bent in case the wind gusts and place your feet on the extreme edges of the board. You should be able to sail for some distance in this position.

5   To catapult the board out of the water step even further back so that the board tilts right up. Then take small quick steps down the board and, before you fall off, push the tail down hard. As you step off the board, let go of the boom and the board will leap out of the water into the air.

Remember . . .
. . . to steer the board by tilting the rails.
. . . that the more of the tail you can drive under the water the higher the board will pop out when you jump off.

This is a neat little trick which can be used in many movements, although it is mostly used when coming out of a **flare gybe** as you are clew first at that point. It is on dry land that you will find out the difficult part of this trick, which is to spin the body and still keep the clew of the sail out of the water.

The object is to sail **clew first** (page 14) and then, letting go of the sail so that it turns downwind, to spin your body 360° and catch the boom as it comes towards you.

Practise sailing clew first across the wind for a reasonable distance. Let go with your sail hand which will allow the clew to be blown downwind. Pull the rig slightly towards you as the sail spins round and grab the boom. Keep practising this until confident.

1   Start in a light wind and sail off on a beam reach, clew first. Then let go of the boom with the leading hand (left hand in this photo sequence).

2   At the same time spin round on the front foot, turning towards the front of the board first.

3   Halfway through the spin pull the mast to windward with your right hand which remains on the boom for this purpose. Let go of the boom and immediately grasp the mast with your left hand. You may need to pull the mast to windward again to keep the clew out.

Mistake: as the boom swings away pull the mast to windward or the clew will hit the water.

4   As you complete the spin pull the rig to windward to keep the clew out of the water. Reach across to the boom with your right hand and continue sailing in the usual way.

Remember . . .
. . . to stop the spin with the back foot.
. . . to pull the rig to windward while spinning.
. . . that having a sail with a high clew helps.

continued overleaf

This is the trick everyone would love to be able to do — if only for a few metres — and is the cornerstone for all difficult tricks being done nowadays.

Railriding must be practised on dry land if only to get the right feel, otherwise one can try for weeks on the water without success. The way to practise this trick on land is described on page 9; don't attempt the trick on water until you can balance the board without support. Make sure the universal joint is hammered tightly into the board before you begin.

The two main ways of getting the board on edge are either by hooking up the windward rail and balancing on it with your front foot, or else by sitting on the rail with your back thigh and placing your front foot on the daggerboard. The latter is the way I explain here.

1 Sail across the wind and practise lifting the windward rail with your front foot on that rail opposite the daggerboard and your back foot on the leeward rail. Tilt the board more as your confidence increases.

2 Move your hands back down the boom. This will keep the rig forward and the board moving in a straight line when on the rail.

3 Continue tilting the board until it comes up against the mast. As it does so, shift your front foot onto the daggerboard (with the side of your foot touching the board) and sit on the rail with the thigh of your other leg.

Your back foot will then rest on the leeward side of the board. Don't sit too far back.

4 Immediately concentrate on the rig. Keep leaning the mast forward to stop the board heading up into the wind. Balance the board on its edge by sheeting in to stop it falling to windward and pressing on the daggerboard to stop it falling to leeward.

5 When you are confident in this position try pulling down on the boom and standing up on your front foot putting your back foot on the rail. Use the back foot to help keep a straight course. Practise sailing like this until you can sail without the board pressing on the mast.

6 Now try placing your front foot on the rail, allowing the board to press on the mast. At this stage it is important to keep your knees bent and your weight low for extra stability.

7 To return to normal sailing push on the daggerboard and pull on the boom.

Remember . . .

. . . to put the universal joint in very tightly, binding the flange with tape if necessary.

. . . a steady force 3 is the ideal wind to give you enough power to do this trick.

Below: a view from the leeward side.

It you feel very wobbly bend your knees to lower your weight.

Steering on the rail: left, to turn away from the wind rake the mast forwards and ease out the boom; centre, sailing straight; right, to turn into the wind rake the mast back and pull in the boom.

This trick is a natural progression from the forwards **railride** which you should master first. You must also learn how to **sail backwards** (page 15) before you begin.

Practise on dry land before you hit the water. It is not possible to tilt the board on its edge on land so have someone hold the board on the rail across the wind. Practise balancing, using your body and the rig until you can balance without support.

1 Sail backwards across the wind on a close reach. Place your front foot (the left foot in the photo sequence) on the leeward side and your right foot on the windward rail opposite the daggerboard case.

2 Practise tilting the board so that the windward rail comes up out of the water.

3 Wait until the stern of the board is turning into the wind, then tilt the board right up so that the windward rail comes up against the mast. At the same time place your right foot on the daggerboard. Sit with your left thigh on the rail.

4 Now the board is on the rail it will start to bear away of its own accord. Practise steering by leaning the mast back to the nose of the board. By putting your weight onto the nose of the board and tilting the board towards the wind you will steer a straight line.

5 When confident step up onto the rail with your left foot by pulling down on the boom and pushing on the daggerboard with your right leg.

6 The last step is to transfer your right foot onto the rail in front of the mast.

Remember . . .
. . . at each stage to practise steering before moving on.
. . . to let the board head up slightly into the wind before finally tilting it onto the rail. Its natural inclination is to bear away (unlike the forwards railride) so this gives more time before you need to make a correction.

I put this trick in as it shows how a combination of simple tricks can be put together to make a difficult trick. You must be able to perform competently each separate trick although in this case the **sail 360** (page 24) is used in a different way. The other tricks you must be sure of are the **clew-first spin** (page 38) and **sailing leeward side of sail** (page 20).

It is useful to try to do all this on dry land first, if only to get the manoeuvre clear in your mind before venturing on the water. A force 2 is about the right wind to start with but as with most tricks it will look more spectacular done in a stronger wind.

The object is to go into a tack but stay on the leeward side of the board for a second. Then move the sail through 360° and spin your body round to continue sailing in the normal position.

1 Lean the mast back as if to go into a tack, but instead of letting go the boom hold onto it and oversheet.

2 Once the board has passed through the wind lean the mast to the front of the board and push the boom away from you. The sail will fill with wind, so lean hard into it to hold it down.

3 Hold this position for a second then push the clew into the wind making sure both feet are behind the mast.

4 Once the clew has been pushed through the wind let go with the sail hand so that the clew is blown downwind.

5 Hold the mast to windward with the mast hand to keep the clew out of the water. Then spin the body on the foot nearest the back of the board in the opposite direction to the sail.

6   When you have spun halfway you will
find the boom in front of you. Grab hold of it
and sail off.

Remember . . .
. . . to lean the mast forward once through the
wind.
. . . to spin as soon as you let go with the
sheet hand so you finish your spin as the
boom swings downwind.

Confidence plays a large part in this trick — a good duck tack looks simple but professional. Ideally you need a force 2 wind and flat water for this trick.

The objective is to tack the board, but instead of going round the front of the mast you throw the rig into the wind and duck underneath the clew of the sail, coming up on the other side as the board completes its tack. Try out the duck tack on dry land by positioning the nose of the board head to wind, then practise throwing the rig into the wind and ducking underneath.

1 Sail across the wind and establish a mark on the horizon where the wind is coming from, so that when it comes to throwing the mast into the wind you'll know where to throw it.

2 Lean the rig back so that the board turns slowly into the wind. Continue holding the rig back until the nose of the board has just passed through the eye of the wind. Now move fast as it's important to keep the board turning through the wind.

3 Throw the rig directly into the wind, let go with your sail hand and slide the mast hand up the boom, grabbing it and giving a sharp tug back towards you.

4 Duck underneath the sail and grab the other side of the boom as close to the mast as possible with your former sail hand. Once both hands are on the boom lean the mast forwards to bear away and pick up speed.

Remember . . .
. . . that once you've thrown the rig forward you must give a sharp tug straight back (a) to stop it going too far forwards, (b) to keep the sail empty of wind — if it fills it will tend to twist around but you want to keep it edge-on to the wind — and (c) to help you grab the boom reasonably far forwards on the new side.
. . . to get the mast directly into the eye of the wind, otherwise the rig will end up in the water.
. . . to get the board slightly through the eye of the wind so that once you have ducked you are ready to sail off.
. . . the better you get the less you need to throw the rig into the wind but the lower you have to duck underneath the sail.

The object is to railride on the leeward rail instead of the more normal windward rail. The leeward railride is more difficult because you have to go from sailing normally to two feet on the rail straight away, instead of building up by first sitting on the rail and then using the daggerboard.

Do not attempt this trick unless you fully understand the principle behind a normal railride (page 39) and can do it competently with two feet up.

1 Sail off on a broad reach and keep the boom well out.

2 Practise tilting the board by depressing the windward rail with your front foot and lifting the leeward rail with your back foot. The instep of the back foot should be squarely on the rail so that it can take your whole weight when you decide to bring the board fully onto the rail.

3 As you practise tilting the board you will notice the nose turning into the wind. If this

happens correct its direction and continue practising just tilting the rail until you can say the board is almost on its rail.

4 When confident, tilt the board fully on its side and — most important — bring your weight over the rail and quickly place your front foot on the rail.

5 The top rail should be brought over to windward so that it rests against the mast. Because you have the boom well out at this stage you can sheet in to help your balance.

6 Once you have the board on the rail with two feet up get it back down flat quickly before you fall off — or go head to wind . . . and then fall off!

Remember . . .
. . . to keep your weight over the board and bend your knees.
. . . to start on a broad reach.
. . . to keep the boom well out to start with.

This trick can be done sailing either forwards or backwards but the principle is the same in both cases. I describe here how to do the trick sailing backwards because although this looks harder in fact it is just the opposite.

You must practise sailing **back to sail** (page 12) until you are confident you can handle both gusts and lulls. While sailing like this practise lifting the daggerboard up 15 cm or so. The water pressure on the daggerboard should keep it in position, but if not use a little tape to build up its sides. Trying the trick on dry land, with the board held firmly on the rail, will give you the feeling of the gusts and is strongly recommended, although getting into the correct position can be tricky.

1   Align the board across the wind with the stern pointing in the direction you want to go. While you are still learning pull the daggerboard a quarter up before stepping back to sail and getting under way.

2   Once you have managed to keep the board in a straight line for a moment, practise tilting the board by depressing the leeward rail with your foot that is furthest from the daggerboard case (the right foot in the photo sequence).

3   As the windward rail comes up lean your body forward and step onto the daggerboard with your left foot. Your right foot now shifts from the leeward side onto the windward rail, although most of your weight is on the left foot.

4   Lean your body to and fro to steer the board. When the wind gusts you should lean forward and twist your body which lets the sail spill wind.

5 When confident try standing between the boom and the sail and then put the board on the rail. However this does require a stronger wind.

Remember . . .
. . . to lean forward onto the daggerboard when on the rail.
. . . to twist your body to sheet out.

Before attempting this trick you must be able to **railride** (page 39) and **sail leeward side of sail** (page 20) facing the sail, because both of these tricks combined with a bit of steering make up this one trick. Tacking on the rail should first be practised on dry land by slotting the board between two trees or posts so it points into the wind, and then trying step 2 (below). A medium wind (force 2 to 3) and flat water are ideal for this trick.

We are trying to go from a normal railride into a tack staying on the rail and finishing on the leeward side of the sail. Note that you do not change your body position during the manoeuvre as you would when tacking.

1   Lean the mast back to turn the board into the wind and if necessary oversheet to keep wind in the sail to give you balance.

2   Keep leaning the mast back until the board is well through the eye of the wind. Then in one swift movement lean the mast to the nose of the board and push away from you with the sail hand until the sail fills and you are on the opposite tack.

3   Do not oversheet with the back hand or the wind won't flow over the sail properly. Balance the board with the shin of your front leg and the instep of your back foot, using the wind pressure on the sail to steady yourself.

4   Keep the mast well forward until you are well under way on the new tack, accentuating it if the nose of the board starts to turn into the wind.

5   When ready flick the rail down and stand on the board, then move to the windward side of the sail and you are ready for your next trick.

Remember . . .
. . . to keep the sail full for as long as possible.
The only moment it should flap is when you
push it through the wind.
. . . wait until the board has turned through
the eye of the wind before pushing the boom
away from you.
. . . don't push the sail hand too far away
when eventually sailing or the sail will stall.
. . . lean the mast far enough forward to stop
the board turning into the wind.

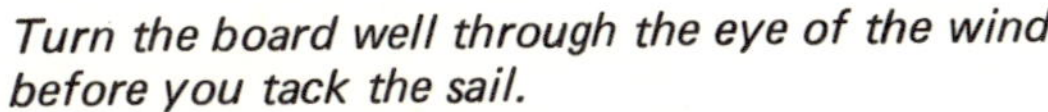

*Turn the board well through the eye of the wind
before you tack the sail.*

51

Here we have a **duck tack** with a 360° spin thrown in as well. To start off it is essential that you can do a confident duck tack (page 46) in almost any conditions. It helps to be able to do a **pirouette** as well because you have to do the spin quickly before the rig is blown back at you.

This is another trick which it is essential to practise on dry land to get the correct body positions. Begin by making the movements slowly but be sure you can complete the trick at a fairly good speed before venturing on the water.

1 Tack the board into the wind as for a duck tack.

2 Throw the rig into the wind but as you duck underneath the sail stop the rig and give a slight tug back with the mast hand which has slid up the boom towards the clew for this purpose.

3 Having ducked right down spin on the front foot in a clockwise direction.

4 Use the back foot to spin the body round and also to check the body after completing the spin.

5 Then reach up and grasp the boom, bear away and sail off.

Remember . . .
. . . that handling the rig properly will give you the time you need to spin.
. . . to keep your body low when spinning.
. . . to handle the trick positively.

Many tricks look terrible if not done properly and this one is no exception; but when done well and with confidence it looks great. The success of the trick can be measured by how much of your body you can get inside the boom while standing on the rail.

The object of the trick is to sail for 20 to 30 metres with the boom against your bottom, your mast hand on the mast well above the boom and standing straight up on the rail. You want to achieve this quickly and not spend time on the rail with your neck against the boom and bottom stuck out to windward.

Trying this one out on dry land is tricky unless the board is held firmly but it is worth the trouble. Before trying to stand inside the boom make sure you can railride two feet up with confidence. A steady force 3 wind is ideal for this trick.

1 Sail on a beam reach on the rail with your back foot on the rail and your front foot on the daggerboard. Then place your mast hand on the mast just below the boom and

reposition your sail hand so it's gripping the boom from the inside.

Mistake: don't sail along with your bottom stuck out —stand up straight as soon as you can.

2   Keep the rig forward at all times to stop the board turning into the wind too quickly.

3   Now bend your head underneath the boom and, when confident, place your front foot on the rail and stand up straight between the sail and the boom.

4   Move your mast hand inside the boom to grab the mast well above the boom.

5   Use your body to control the sheeting in and out of the boom. For stability keep the board pressed against the mast at all times.

6   To get out of this position simply let the board fall down flat by pulling it with your feet and either continue sailing between the boom and sail or duck your head and let the boom pass over.

Remember . . .

. . . don't pause when your head and neck are between the boom and sail but immediately try to stand up straight on the rail.

. . . the sail hand stays in the same place throughout the trick.

Mistake: keep the board pressed against the mast — and don't oversheet.

Water starting onto the rail with the daggerboard in place is a fairly common freestyle trick; but it can also be done without the daggerboard as I discovered in a flash of inspiration during the Windsurfer Worlds in Japan. During my compulsory routine I fell off to windward from a railride with the daggerboard out and managed to water start back onto the rail still clutching my daggerboard.

Do not attempt this trick unless you can do both an ordinary **water start** (page 34) and a **railride** (page 39). Unfortunately it is impossible to practise on dry land. You need a force 4 to 5 wind and a tight universal joint.

1   Point the board across the wind and lower yourself into the water as for a normal water start.

2   Shift your calves onto the board and hook the windward rail right under your bottom.

3   Depress the leeward rail with your heels and lift the windward rail with your thighs. The windward rail will now come up against the mast and you'll find yourself sitting on the rail.

4   Transfer your front foot onto the rail keeping the board and mast touching. Push up on the front foot bringing the back foot onto the rail at the same time.

5   What happens next depends on whether you have the daggerboard hanging on your arm or in its slot. If the daggerboard is in its slot place your front foot on it as for normal railriding (as in the photo sequence) and move on to other tricks. If the daggerboard is out, see how upright you can stand on the rail. Finally flip the board flat and put the daggerboard in again.

Remember . . .
. . . to keep your weight low.
. . . to have a tight universal joint.
. . . to help the water start onto the rail by letting the rig catch more wind.
. . . you must keep the board right against the mast because without the braking force of the daggerboard the windward rail will tend to fall quickly.

29 Everole

In this trick the board is sailed upside down with the sailor standing on the bottom. It sounds hard to believe but if you can do a decent **railride** and sail **clew first** you are well on your way to learning this trick. It is named after Gary Eversole, an innovative American freestylist, and as you will see this is a highly innovative trick.

Practise a clew-first railride until you are completely confident as this leads into an Everole. It is very important that the flange of the universal joint is wrapped in plenty of tape and literally hammered in place to withstand the pressure of the board on the mast.

The Everole from another angle.

1 Point the nose of the board almost onto a broad reach. Swivel the sail round so that you are sailing clew first and put the board on the rail leaving the front foot on the daggerboard.

2 Move your hands up towards the clew of the sail and place the sole of your front foot half on the bottom of the board and half on the daggerboard keeping your toes pointing towards the front of the board.

3 By tilting the upper rail to leeward and against the mast with your back foot you will turn the board upside down.

4 There are three ways of controlling the position of your board: (a) by using the pressure of your back foot, (b) by the front foot pressing either on the daggerboard or on

the bottom of the board and (c) by pulling the mast towards you which will bring up the rail. If you want the board to sail flatter let the mast fall to leeward.

5 Keep practising until you can steer the board and stop it luffing up. Once you have sailed upside down for some distance bring the board back onto the rail by pulling on the mast and continue sailing on the rail.

Remember . . .
. . .don't go into the Everole from a railride unless you are still pointing on a beam reach.
. . . to move your hands towards the clew of the sail before flattening the board.
. . . to make the universal joint really tight.

Although an easy trick to describe this is extremely difficult to execute. You must practise this on dry land. I rigged up a mast horizontally at boom height between two supports in the garden and practised flipping round it until I got the feel of it. Cushions on the ground will protect you from injury.

The object is to fling your legs up through the gap between the boom and the sail, following with your body and somersaulting back onto the board. Usually, however, you finish up in the water so it's best to make this your final trick; if you do land back on the board you'll gain valuable points but if you splash down it's still a spectacular finish. A wide boom will give more room for your body when flipping. A small body will help even more!

1 Sail across the wind in a force 4 and hold the boom with your hands underneath and fairly wide apart.

2 Let the rig fall to leeward slightly so that when you put all your weight on the rig during the flip you will pull it back to its original position instead of into the water.

3 When ready, push off on one foot and swing both feet up between the boom and sail.

4 Swing on the boom and try to bring your feet back onto the board.

Remember . . .

. . . to lean the rig to leeward.

. . . really go for it — and practise on dry land first.

A freestyle programme

Here are some points to bear in mind when planning a three-minute freestyle routine.

Only do tricks you are 90 per cent certain will come off. Do the easiest tricks first to gain confidence (and points), leaving the harder tricks till later, preferably ending with something really difficult — the audience will expect a final splash!

Your sequence of tricks must flow — like a snooker player the end of one trick must leave you in position to begin the next. Practise your routine in segments; then put all the segments together to make the whole show.

Practise in all conditions. In a blow, the tricks happen so fast you may run out of things to do before the three minutes are up — so take your time. Concentrate on the easier tricks like the flare gybe and water start and avoid tough manoeuvres like the Everole. In a drifter your routine tends to look boring — so pack in the action even if it means repeating tricks several times.

If you are a beginner, work out a sequence and stick to it. If you are more experienced, plan the first minute and a half and then improvise until the end. In this way you are certain to amass a lot of points early on, leaving room for a brilliant finale!

The sequence I usually follow for the first part of the routine is shown below.

Finally, if you are in a good position in the competition overall, do a conservative routine. If you're down the pan, go for it and don't worry about falling in (especially if you can do a water start!).

start	sail 360	pirouette	body & sail 360	flare gybe
flare gybe & half turn	back to sail & back to sail inside boom	duck tack	railride	railride 2 feet up

The judge's point of view

by Alex Schatunowski

Having managed to master some of the tricks in this book, you may consider — either by choice or more probably bullying by your club mates — entering your first freestyle event. Knowing your tricks and being able to do them in your own time and on your own water is one thing, but being able to put together a flowing and graceful routine is something completely different. This section of the book looks at the freestyle competition from the judge's point of view — what the judge is looking for in a routine, and how you can produce the necessary goods.

Competition requirements. In most freestyle events each competitor presents a routine lasting three minutes. This may not seem long, but when you are out there trying to remember which trick you haven't already done, it can seem like a lifetime. Many competitions run eliminating rounds requiring only a two-minute routine.

Competitors are judged individually, the order of competition being decided beforehand usually by a standard draw. Throughout the routine timing and signals are important and most competitions will specify these in their instructions. There is generally a preparatory signal indicating that the judges are ready, and you are required to drop your hand or provide some other clear signal to mark the start of your routine, which will be the time that the clock starts. There will often be a further sound signal after two and a half minutes, with a penultimate signal ten seconds before the end of the routine. Try to time your final, spectacular trick to coincide with the end of the countdown, leaving the maximum impact in the judges' minds.

Preparation. Before going out on the water to compete, study the area of the competition. In particular, check the mean wind direction and search out the wind shadows and holes. Try to establish also whether there are any regular gusts and their general direction; there is nothing more likely to mess up your best trick than a misjudged untimely gust. Perhaps most important of all, find out where the judges will be positioned.

Throughout your routine, remember to play to the judges. Stay reasonably close to them, particularly when you are performing your best tricks. Think also about the wind direction in relation to the judges' position, especially if you find it easier to perform certain tricks on one or the other tack. It is most frustrating to complete one of your most spectacular tricks and discover that the sail has been between you and the judges throughout. Whatever your egotistical tendencies may be, do not perform to the cameras. They don't award points and their job is after all to photograph you rather than you posing for them.

Scoring. Most important is to know what the judges are going to be looking for throughout your performance. Judging techniques and standards obviously vary tremendously, but generally points will be awarded in the following categories:

1 Number of tricks   20
2 Difficulty of tricks   25
3 Execution of tricks   25
4 Overall impression of routine 30

The total points awarded against each of these categories may also vary (although the split shown above is typical) and you should be advised before the competition what these will be.

Number of tricks. This carries 20 points on the basis of one point per trick satisfactorily completed, and you should always aim to

achieve maximum points. As you only receive
one point per trick, never repeat tricks unless
they are essential to maintain flow in a section
of related tricks. Those of you competing in
the primary or intermediate levels can achieve
points by performing variations on a number
of basic tricks. If we consider a back-to-sail
position, a variation could be sailing inside
the boom and even clapping your hands. Basic
sail tricks have many variations and you may
be well advised to spend the first one to one-
and-a-half minutes going through as many
tricks as possible, including all the easy ones,
and collecting a respectable number of points,
particularly if you spend no more than a few
seconds in each different sailing position.

Difficulty of tricks. The types of trick you
attempt will depend upon your own expertise
and, more importantly, the wind strength.
Every freestylist has his or her favourite wind
strength and a force above or below this can
seriously affect a strictly rigid routine, so try
to maintain some flexibility to take this into
account and attempt tricks you are reasonably
confident of performing for a given wind
strength — nothing wastes more time than
getting under way again once in the water,
and a fall can seriously affect both your
concentration and confidence. A moderately
difficult trick well executed will gain more
points than a difficult trick that fails, particularly if a penalty system is in force.

If you are confident on the rail, don't be
satisfied with just sailing off into the distance.
Show the judges that you are as confident on
the rail as you are on the board sailed flat
and remember all the variations on a basic
railride — forwards, backwards, clew first,
both feet on the rail, sitting on the rail, even
lying on the rail. This not only demonstrates
expertise and confidence but also gains points
for the number of tricks completed.

In some competitions, a tariff system may
be set out with different tariff points for
moderate or high wind. Examples of the more
difficult type of trick, in order of difficulty,
which may be compulsory in some compe-

titions are head dip, sail 360, railride, nose dip,
duck tack, pirouette and spin tack. Try to put
in some difficult tricks towards the end of
your routine as judges generally finalise their
marks at that stage and the latter part is likely
to be fresh in their minds.

Execution of tricks. This category carries
comparatively high points and the judges will
mark you on your execution of each trick. So
perform every trick to your best ability,
exercising poise and flair. Simple things count,
such as the outstretched rear arm with straight
fingers during a duck tack. Try the odd cheeky
move. For example, if you manage to perform
a trick standing only on one foot, use the
other foot to paddle a couple of times through
the water.

If one of your tricks for any reason fails
and you are still confident you can do it,
attempt it again, especially if it is part of a
good continuity routine. This is particularly
relevant if penalty points are in force as a fall
could incur three penalty points, yet if you
perform the trick successfully you should be
able to pick up more than three points from
the 50 maximum points available for difficulty
and execution.

Overall impression. This is judged purely on
the basis of what you have actually performed
and not on what you have omitted. If the
general standard of competition is high with
other competitors performing many difficult
tricks, you will obviously be down on points
for those sections. However, even a relatively
simple routine can score high points in this
section if the routine as a whole is polished
and well presented.

The planning of your routine can help
maximise on points in this category. Some
reasonably simple tricks are perfect to use as
links to help the flow from one difficult
trick to another. For example, 180° sail
turns are most effective in providing continuity
in a series of related tricks. A very popular
combination is normal sailing to clew first,
stepping around the front to leeside back to

sail and finishing with a sail spin-out back to
the normal position. A duck tack could, if
necessary, bring you back towards the judges
bearing away slightly for a forwards railride,
board 180, backwards railride, then flare
gybe.

Before the event, plan your routine on
paper, with tacks and gybes sensibly integrated
to keep you within easy visible distance of
the judges rather than sailing off into the
distance. At the Windsurfer Europeans in
1981, one particularly good competitor
sailed so far on one tack that only the use of
binoculars could distinguish what he was
actually doing and valuable points were lost.

Always complete your routine with a care-
fully planned final combination. If you have a
mental clock, that's fine, but if not, try to
work out a 25-second combination that you
can put into effect within several seconds of
the two-and-a-half minutes sailed signal. In
planning this routine, try to include difficult
tricks that you are confident of completing —
do not risk a fall. You can even afford to
repeat a trick if it forms an integral part of
this final routine, building up towards your
dismount which should be timed to coincide
with the final signal.

A backwards flip through the boom is
excellent if you manage to land back on the
board, but this is a particularly difficult
trick and if you are fairly certain you will
land in the water, just try to ensure that the
final gun fires while you are in the air. Similarly
a nose sink/tail sink, preferably on the rail,
should be timed to catch the board in the air
on the gun. Your dismount can either be
spectacular or calculatingly cool, like Dee
Caldwell sailing up the beach in the 1981

Windsurfer Europeans right in front of the
judges and stepping calmly onto the sand just
as the gun fired.

Penalties. A penalty system has been used in
the UK at a number of events since early 1981
and this system was also introduced at the
1981 Windsurfer European Freestyle Cham-
pionship. Penalties are awarded on the following basis:

Fall in the water — 3 penalty points
Fall onto the board — 2 penalty points
Drop rig — 2 penalty points
Drag the clew of the sail — 1 penalty point

The organisers felt that the introduction of
penalty points would ensure competitors
maintained maximum concentration and
attention to detail, but obviously the judges
must exercise discretion as there are some
tricks (for example) that are difficult to
perform without the clew touching the water.
Many of the competitors were disturbed by
the introduction of penalty points, but having
adjudicated in these competitions, I am quite
satisfied that recording penalties on the judging
sheet does assist the judge in assessing an overall impression once the routine is complete
and, after all, the winners of these events will
always be the ones that commit the least
number of errors.

It is argued by some that penalty points
would discourage competitors from attempting
particularly difficult tricks for fear of incurring
penalties, but a mistake is nonetheless a
mistake and marking down a competitor on
the basis of penalty points is merely a more
accurate way of recording imperfections in
the routine in a job which is primarily most
subjective.